BUILDING A
Dams

Chris Oxlade

Heinemann
LIBRARY

H www.heinemann.co.uk
Visit our website to find out more information about Heinemann Library books.

To order:
☎ Phone 44 (0) 1865 888066
🖹 Send a fax to 44 (0) 1865 314091
💻 Visit the Heinemann Bookshop at www.heinemann.co.uk to browse our catalogue and order online.

First published in Great Britain by Heinemann Library, Halley Court, Jordan Hill, Oxford OX2 8EJ
a division of Reed Educational and Professional Publishing Ltd.
Heinemann is a registered trademark of Reed Educational & Professional Publishing Ltd.

OXFORD MELBOURNE AUCKLAND JOHANNESBURG BLANTYRE
GABORONE IBADAN PORTSMOUTH (NH) USA CHICAGO

Designed by Celia Floyd
Illustrations by Barry Atkinson and Jeff Edwards
Originated by Repro Multi Warna
Printed by Wing King Tong in Hong Kong

ISBN 0 431 10976 1 (hardback)   ISBN 0 431 10983 4 (paperback)
05 04 03 02 01   05 04 03 02 01
10 9 8 7 6 5 4 3 2 1   10 9 8 7 6 5 4 3 2 1

British Library Cataloguing in Publication Data

Oxlade, Chris
    Dams. – (Building amazing structures)
    1. Dams – Design and construction – Juvenile literature
    I. Title
    627.8

Acknowledgements
The Publishers would like to thank the following for permission to reproduce photographs:
Ancient Art and Architecture Collection p. 6; Bill Hughes p. 20; Corbis pp. 5, 29; Environmental Images p. 26 (Alex Smailes), p. 22 (Omar Sattaur), p. 27 (Toby Adamson); Hutchison Library pp. 16, 18, 23, pp. 12, 19 (Robert Aberman); J Allan Cash pp. 7, 8, 17; James Davis Photography p. 11; KATZ p. 15; Tony Stone p. 25 (Ary Diesendruck), p. 10 (Chris Swartz), p. 4 (Peter/Steff Lamberti).

Cover photograph reproduced with permission of Tony Stone.

Every effort has been made to contact copyright holders of any material reproduced in this book. Any omissions will be rectified in subsequent printings if notice is given to the Publisher.

Words appearing in the text in bold, **like this**, are explained in the Glossary.

Contents

About dams

A dam is a huge barrier across a river that blocks the flow of river water. The water builds up behind the dam, making an artificial lake called a **reservoir**.

A dam is a type of structure. A structure is a thing that is built to resist a push or pull. A dam is a structure because it supports the immense wall of water in the reservoir behind it.

The biggest structures ever built are dams. Some are as high as a skyscraper, or as heavy as a mountain, some make reservoirs as big as seas, and some make enough electricity for whole cities.

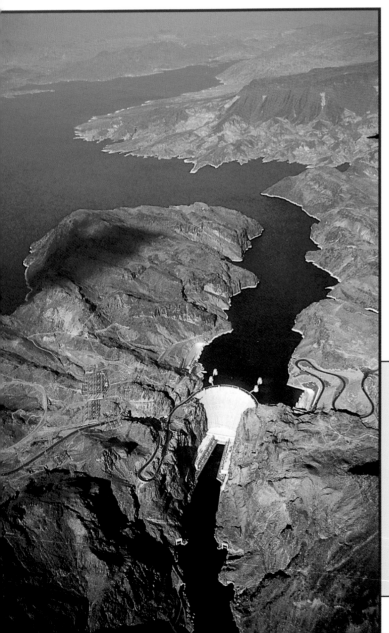

So why do we build dams? What different types of dam are there? How are they built? What special materials and machinery are needed?

Here we see the 221-m-high concrete **arch** of the Hoover Dam, and Lake Mead, the reservoir behind it. They are on the Colorado River, on the Arizona-Nevada border, USA.

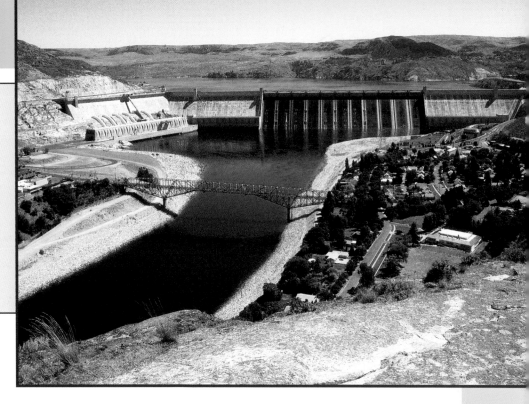

The Grand Coulee Dam in the USA is a large concrete dam. Its hydro-electric power station is on the left.

Why do we build dams?

All dams do the same job, which is to hold back water. Sometimes the water is used for water supply and **irrigation**. Sometimes the water is used to produce electricity for homes, offices and industry. The water flows down from the reservoir into a **hydro-electric power** station, where it turns **turbines** and **generators** that produce electricity.

Some dams are built to stop flooding around a river **downstream** of the dam during heavy rains. The great rush of flood water collects behind the dam and is released gradually into the river below the dam. Some dams are designed to make a river deeper, so that ships can travel up and down the river.

FACTS ✤ It's a world record!

- Highest dam – Rogun Dam, River Vakhsh, Tajikistan. Originally designed to be 335 m high, that's just 50 m shorter than the Empire State Building! Not yet completed due to the break up of the Soviet Union.

- Biggest dam (the dam with the highest volume of material in its structure) – Syncrude **Tailings**, Alberta, Canada. Completed: 1992. Volume: 540,000,000 cubic m. That's enough material to make a heap nearly 3 km high!

5

Dams in the past

People have been building dams for thousands of years. Early dams were built in countries with very dry **climates**. They supplied water to growing cities and **irrigated** land so that more food could be grown for increasing populations. Huge **hydro-electric power** dams have only been built in the last hundred years.

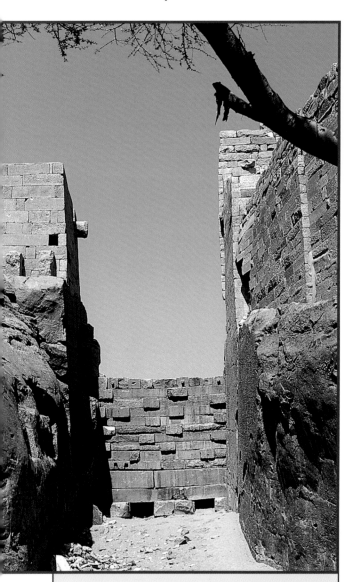

This is a water outlet gate on an 8th-century dam in the Yemen. The dam wall is built from stone blocks.

Ancient dam builders

The Ancient Egyptians probably built the first dams more than 5000 years ago across the River Nile. Later civilizations, such as the **Babylonians** and **Assyrians**, who lived in the area we now call the Middle East, also built dams. So did the Romans. These dams were heavy banks up to 30 m high. They were made of vast amounts of earth or rock – and built without modern machinery. Some used simple concrete for strength and waterproofing. Dam building also started in China and other parts of Asia more than 2000 years ago.

New dams for new industries

In Northern Europe a few dams were built after the **Middle Ages** to supply water to towns, to water-powered mills and to canals. Then in the 18th century came the **Industrial Revolution** and huge quantities of water were needed for rapidly growing cities and new industries.

In the 19th century, **engineers** began to study how structures stay up. New materials, such as stronger **cements** and **reinforced concrete**, were developed and powered tools were invented. This allowed much larger dams to be constructed safely, which could hold back **reservoirs** big enough to supply all the water that was needed.

This dam in Wales is one of the several 19th-century dams that supply water to the cities of central Britain.

FACTS ✛ Old dam details

- The first dam we know of was built in about 2900 BC to divert water from the River Nile, in Egypt, for irrigation.
- The oldest dam still in use is a dam built from rocks about 7 m high in Syria. It was built in about 1300 BC – 3300 years ago.
- The first hydro-electric power station was built at Appleton in Wisconsin, USA, in 1882. Its electricity lit two mills and a house.

Types of dam

Modern dams come in dozens of different shapes and sizes, but there are really only four types. Each resists the push from the water on its **upstream** face in a different way. At the bottom of a **reservoir** 100 m deep, the push on the dam wall is about the same as you would feel if a family car was resting on the palm of your hand!

Gravity dams

Put simply, a **gravity** dam is just an enormously heavy wall of concrete. The immense weight of the water cannot push the dam along or topple it over. The Grand Coulee Dam in Washington State, USA, contains a staggering 20 million tonnes of concrete.

Arch dams

An **arch** dam has a thin concrete wall which curves out into the reservoir. The push of the water goes around the dam to the sides and into the valley sides.

Many dams, such as this one in Nigeria, are made up of different types of dam joined end to end. This dam has an embankment dam at each end, and a gravity dam in the centre.

There are four main types of dam.

GRAVITY DAM — concrete wall

BUTTRESS DAM — buttress

ARCH DAM — curved concrete wall

EMBANKMENT DAM — waterproof layer of earth and rock

Buttress dams

A **buttress** dam has a sloping upstream face. The water pushes downwards and forwards on the face. The downwards push presses the dam into the ground, which helps it resist the forwards push. Heavy walls called buttresses support the **downstream** face to stop the dam toppling over.

Embankment dams

An **embankment** dam is a huge earth or rock bank, with gently sloping faces. It works like a combined gravity and buttress dam, but needs to be many times thicker than both. Earth and rock are not watertight like concrete, so an embankment dam needs a layer of waterproof material on the upstream face, or inside, to stop water seeping through.

TRY THIS
Feel the force
Stand two empty boxes on a flat surface about 10 cm apart. Put a plastic bag between the boxes. Slowly pour water into the bag. Eventually the boxes will move because of the push of the water. You can feel the push by trying to move the boxes together again. The deeper the water in the bag, the bigger the push will be.

Parts of a dam

The main part of every dam is the dam wall itself, which holds back the water in the **reservoir**. The wall is normally quite a simple structure, made from **reinforced concrete**, earth or rock. Other parts of a dam control the flow of water from the reservoir into the river **downstream** of the dam, into water supply pipes or into a **hydro-electric power** station (which is often part of the dam structure, too).

Monster water chutes

All dams have a **spillway** which works like a safety valve, letting water out of the reservoir if the water level rises too high. If there was no spillway, the water would eventually flow over the top of the dam and cascade down the downstream face. This would **erode** the base of the dam, perhaps causing it to collapse.

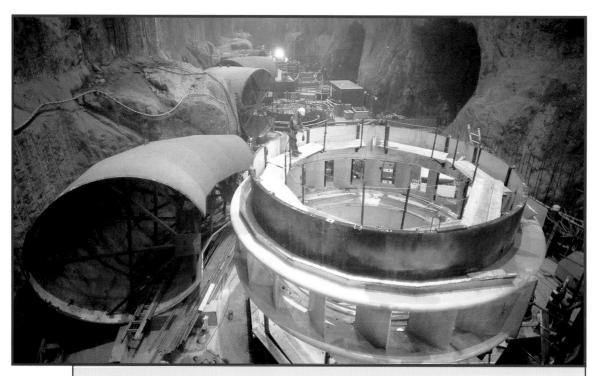

Some dams have a huge **turbine** hall in a cave blasted out of solid rock. Here turbines are being installed.

Spillways like these on the Itaipu Dam, on the Brazil-Paraguay border, handle the equivalent of several swimming pools of water every second, travelling at up to 100 km per hour.

The spillway is either a channel in the downstream face of the dam, a channel at the side of the dam, called a chute, or tunnels blasted through the rock next to the dam.

Supplying water

Dams always have a system of pipes which allow water from the reservoir to flow straight into the river downstream, into the water supply system, **irrigation** channels, or a hydro-electric power station. The inlets to this system are called intakes.

Bypassing the dam

A dam obviously blocks the river, stopping craft from moving along it. Where the river is an important waterway, canal **locks** are built to allow ships to move between the river below the dam and the new reservoir. Some dams also have a series of pools called a fish ladder, which allows fish to bypass the dam by leaping from pool to pool.

Holding up the dam

All dams must have solid foundations to support their massive weight. The foundations are normally made of **bedrock**. Although rocks are solid, most of them do let water seep through, sometimes through cracks and sometimes between the small particles which make up the rock. To stop water seeping through the rock foundations, a dam has a waterproof barrier underneath called a **cut-off**, often made with **grout**.

Dam-building materials

The most important material for modern dam-building is concrete. The ingredients of concrete are **cement**, water and aggregate, which is a mixture of sand and gravel. When the ingredients are first mixed, the concrete is liquid. The cement reacts with the water and then hardens into a solid which holds the aggregate together. Concrete is good for building because it is cheap and enormously strong. In fact, a piece of concrete about 10 cm square could support a 30-tonne weight. Concrete can easily be shaped by pouring it into moulds before it sets.

Reinforced concrete and steel are used to build a water intake on a dam in Turkey.

Adding super-strong steel

Concrete is extremely strong when it is squashed, or compressed. But when stretched, it cracks quite easily. Steel is immensely strong when it is stretched. For example, a steel cable only as thick as your finger could lift a 30-tonne weight. Where part of a concrete structure will be stretched, steel bars are added to it. The new material is called **reinforced concrete**.

Watertight

Dam-builders often need to use special types of cement in their concrete to make it waterproof and stop **seepage**, or to make it resistant to attack by chemicals in the river water. Cement and water are also used to make a material called **grout**.

Looking at seepage

Put a layer of sand about 1 cm thick in the bottom of a tray. Use more sand to build up a model valley. Put a block of wood across the valley to act as a dam. Pour water onto the sand behind the dam to make a reservoir. Can you see how the water seeps through the sand under the wood to the other side? This is what would happen to a dam if the ground underneath was not grouted.

woodblock

sand

Natural materials

Embankment dams are built from materials such as chunks of solid rock, gravel, sand or clay. Materials with very small particles, such as clay, are used as a waterproofing layer.

This is a cross-section of an embankment dam showing the waterproofing structure.

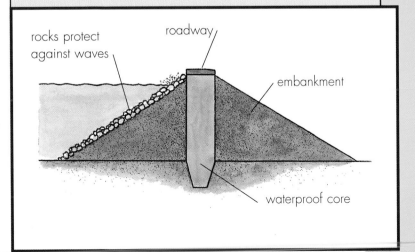

rocks protect against waves

roadway

embankment

waterproof core

Designing a dam

Dams are built for large organizations. For example, an electricity supply company might want to build a dam to generate electricity, or a water supply company might want to build a dam to provide extra water. They hire a team of **engineers** to work on the design and construction of the dam. A **consulting engineer** oversees the project.

How big?

The engineers need to think about many different factors before deciding on the size of the dam. For example, if the dam is to produce electricity, it must be high so that the **reservoir** is deep and water rushes into the **turbines** with plenty of energy. These are called **hydro-electric** dams. If the dam is for water supply or flood control, the dam can be lower and longer so that it creates a large reservoir.

Where to build?

The site chosen will depend on its suitability for the construction of the dam itself and on the effects the reservoir will have when it is full of water. A **geological survey** of the ground around the site will tell the engineers whether the ground will support

What if an earthquake strikes?

Designers always investigate the **seismic** activity of a dam site. Earthquakes can crack a dam, making it leak or even collapse, and cause catastrophic flooding. Computer simulations (tests on a computerized model of the dam) help engineers tell what would happen if an earthquake struck a dam they are designing.

the weight of the dam and whether the rock is waterproof. The survey is done by digging **boreholes** to get samples of rock from deep underground.

What sort of dam?

The type of dam chosen depends on the width and depth of the valley and the **geology** of the site. **Embankment** dams are normally built in broad valleys where the **bedrock** is buried under layers of soft ground such as **silt** and clay, and where the cost of a concrete dam would be too high. Concrete dams are normally built in narrow valleys where the bedrock is near the surface.

This is a model of the design of the Three Gorges Dam in China. Models like this help engineers to explain the structure and workings of the proposed dam to non-engineers.

Preparing the ground

Building a large dam is an enormous undertaking which can take thousands of workers more than ten years to complete. Usually one **engineering** company organizes the whole construction job. The dozens of special jobs, such as **grouting**, pipe work, or fixing steel reinforcements, are carried out by smaller companies.

Going underground

There is normally a lot of digging to do. Loose earth and rock must be removed to reveal the solid rocks that will form the foundations for the heavy dam. Trenches may need to be excavated to install waterproof **cut-offs** under the ground. If the rock allows water to seep through, holes are drilled and grout is pumped down them, from where it spreads into the ground and sets.

Before digging starts, a channel or tunnel is dug around the side of the site and the river is diverted to flow through it.

On the Itaipu Dam on the Brazil-Paraguay border, 50 million tonnes of rock had to be dug up just to create a diversion channel for the river.

Earth-moving monsters

Giant earth-moving machines do the digging work. Excavators dig down into the ground with a room-sized bucket, pulling up more earth in one go than a person could shovel in day. Bulldozers push loose earth and rock about, and loaders pick it up and drop it into dump trucks – massive trucks as high as houses. Where solid rock needs to be removed, it is broken up with explosives first.

These loaders and trucks are moving earth and rock at the site of the Gubi Dam in Nigeria.

TRY THIS

Firm foundations

Fill a container, such as a large margarine tub, with sand or earth and smooth the top over. Put the tub outdoors. Stand an empty plastic bottle on top of the sand. Gradually fill the bottle with water. As the bottle becomes heavier, the sand settles under it. This is what happens under a concrete dam as more and more concrete is added.

Building the dam

Once the ground works are completed, work on the structure of the dam itself can begin. Large concrete dams contain a mind-boggling amount of concrete. Thirty million tonnes of it in the case of the Itaipu Dam on the Brazil-Paraguay border. Delivering this much **ready-mixed concrete** would have taken two trucks working every minute of every day for a whole year. So concrete-making plants are built at the site, and the concrete is carried into place in containers hanging from overhead cables. As the dam wall itself goes up, other parts of the dam, such as the **spillways** and **hydro-electric power** station, are constructed too.

Concrete and more concrete

Before any concrete is mixed, a mould must be made for it to be poured into. The mould is made with wooden sheets or

steel plates, called **formwork**, supported by scaffolding. The reinforcing steel is put in place so that it will be encased when the concrete sets. The formwork stays in place until the concrete is set.

A concrete dam is built up in layers, and each layer is allowed to set before the next is added. The concrete is also covered with plastic sheeting to stop it drying too quickly, which would make it crack.

Reinforcing steel and formwork can be seen at the top of this concrete dam wall.

Moving the earth

Millions of tonnes of earth and rock are needed to build an **embankment** dam, and dozens of massive earth-moving machines are needed. Earth and rock are quarried, transported to the site in monster trucks and tipped on the embankment. Each fresh layer is compacted (pressed down firmly) by heavy rolling machines to make it more waterproof and to stop it from being squashed by the weight of the layers above.

As the embankment rises, rocks or concrete blocks, often as big as cars, are added to the **upstream** face to protect it from the waves.

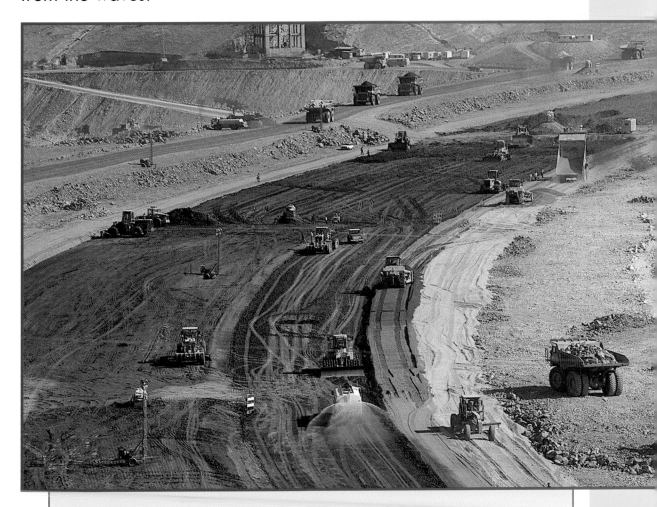

The gigantic earth embankment of the Ataturk Dam in Turkey is built up by earth-moving machines.

Dams in use

With the dam complete, the **reservoir** begins to fill with river water. It may take months or even years to reach its full depth. Then the dam can begin supplying water and producing electricity. Some reservoirs are also used for leisure activities, such as fishing or sailing.

Controlling the flow

Hydrologists (experts on how water is collected and used) control how the water flows out of the reservoir. They operate sluice gates which allow water into water supply pipes, or the **hydro-electric power** station, or straight into the river below the dam.

On the Akosomba Dam in Ghana, water flows downstream down huge pipes on the face, to the power station at the base of the dam.

Clearing the river

Allowing enough water into the river is important for the life in it and along its banks. It also stops the river from filling up with **silt.** Silt, or sediment, can build up because a dam reduces the natural flow of water. The slower the water flow, the more likely it is that silt will build up in the river channel. Occasionally a great rush of water is released to create a flood **downstream**. This helps to clear the river of silt.

Silt also settles at the bottom of the reservoir, leaving less room for the water. Most silt comes down the river during floods, so flood water is often allowed to flow out of the dam before the silt settles.

Spotting the cracks

A dam collapse can be a catastrophe because the whole reservoir full of water is released in one go. So the structure of a dam is constantly checked to make sure it is not moving or cracking. This is most important during the first few years after it has been completed. The ground under the dam and the reservoir can shift because of the added weight on top of it. Instruments inside the dam measure the forces on the dam and detect any tiny movements. The instruments can also tell designers if the structure is working as they thought it would.

TRY THIS

Taming a flood

This simple experiment shows how a finished dam helps with flood protection (see page 5) by storing a rush of flood water and releasing it gradually. Prop up one corner of a large, deep tray (such as a roasting tin) so that this corner is a few centimetres higher than the opposite corner. Fill the tray with water until it overflows at the lowest corner. This represents a full reservoir. Now quickly pour a cup of 'flood water' into the top corner. You should see that the water flows out of the bottom corner, but much more slowly.

flood water

reservoir

water released slowly

Dam schemes

In the second half of the 20th century, hundreds of gigantic 'superdams' were built on the major rivers of the world. These dams give huge benefits. They create reliable water supplies for cities and for farmers to grow their crops. They protect against floods and make the electricity needed for homes and industries. But these large dams may not be the best answer. **Environmentalists** argue that large dams do more harm than good because they destroy the natural flow of the river.

Anti-dam groups have tried to stop the construction of India's Sardar Sarovar Dam.

Problems at the Aswan Dam

The Aswan High Dam, in Egypt, was built during the 1960s and 1970s to supply water to **irrigate** new farmland and to produce electricity. The dam cost about a billion US dollars and took more than ten years to build. It is an **embankment** dam 111 m high, 3.9 km long, and nearly 1 km wide at its base. It contains enough rock to build 55 Great Pyramids. The dam's **reservoir**, Lake Nasser, is 22 km across and almost 500 km long. It contains enough water to fill a line of swimming pools 1.5 million km long!

This massive embankment of the Aswan Dam has a **hydro-electric power** station on the far side.

By the 1980s, the farmers were using water from Lake Nasser to grow twice the amount of crops than before the dam was built, and the dam was creating a quarter of Egypt's electricity. A thriving fishing industry had grown up on Lake Nasser.

But the dam has had serious effects on the Nile **downstream**. **Nutritious silt** collects in Lake Nasser and no longer reaches the fields. Farmers have to use thousands of tonnes of artificial **fertilizers** instead, which have contaminated the river water, affecting fish and other life in the river. The Nile **Delta**, which was built up by silt from the river, is being flooded by the sea, and precious farmland is being lost.

This is a map of the River Nile in Egypt, showing the Aswan Dam and Lake Nasser in the south, and the Nile Delta in the north.

23

Flood defences

Structures like dams help to prevent flooding of the low-lying land next to rivers and along the coast. These flood-defence barriers are for keeping water out rather than for keeping it in.

Levees and dykes

Levees are **embankments** built alongside rivers to stop water spilling over the banks when the river level rises as flood water flows down it. Dykes are similar, but protect low-lying coastal land from flooding by the sea. Levees and dykes are normally made of earth and are not more than a few metres high. They must stand up to **erosion** from flowing water and waves.

Dykes are often used to reclaim land from the sea. A dyke is built next to the coast to enclose an area of the sea. Then the sea water is pumped out, leaving a new area of land called a polder.

Turning the tide

Low-lying areas of land near coasts are threatened by storm tides, when the sea rises far above its normal level. A storm tide happens when there is a storm blowing towards the coast at the same time as there is a very high tide. Some coastal areas are protected by sea barriers, which stop storm surges flowing up **estuaries** and rivers.

A barrier has gates which are normally wide open, allowing river water to flow down to the sea, and sea water to flow in, as would happen naturally. But if a storm tide is forecast the gates are closed against it, keeping the rising sea water out.

Power from the tide

A tidal barrage is like a two-way **hydro-electric power** dam across an estuary. As the tide rises, the water is deeper on the seaward side of the barrier. It flows through **turbines**, creating electricity. As the tide falls, the water flows back to the sea, creating electricity again.

A tidal barrage creates power as sea water flows backwards and forwards through its turbines.

The Thames Barrier prevents flooding in low-lying areas of London. The underwater gates can be closed if there is a risk of flooding.

Dams that went wrong

Ever since dams began to be built, some have collapsed, although this very rarely happens to large modern dams. When a dam collapses, the surge of water into the valley below is extremely destructive. Early dams, built mainly of earth, were often washed away as flood water flowed over the top. Others cracked during earthquakes. Modern dams are designed to withstand earthquakes and to let flood water through before it can flow over the top of the dam, but things can still go wrong.

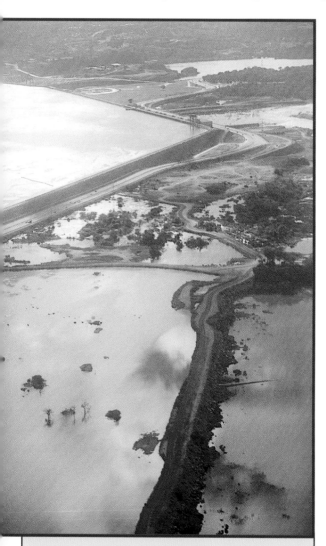

The Guri Dam in Venezuela has not managed to prevent flooding of the surrounding countryside.

Calamitous collapses

The St Francis Dam was a **gravity** dam in the San Francisquito Valley, California, USA, completed in 1926. It collapsed two years later as the **reservoir** filled and pressure on the dam increased. Between 300 and 500 people were killed in the floods. The dam had been built on unstable rock which moved because of the weight of the dam.

In 1975, the Banqiao Dam and Shimantam Dam, both in Henan Province, China, collapsed. It is thought that 230,000 people died because of flooding, famine and disease after the dams collapsed.

Killer wave

The 258-m-high Vaiont Dam in the Italian Alps was completed in 1960. In 1963, flood water filled the reservoir to within 12 m of the top of the dam. When a huge piece of mountain-side above the reservoir slid into the water, it sent a monster wave as high as a 30-storey building across the reservoir and over the dam. The water rushed down the valley below, flooding villages and drowning 2500 people. Amazingly the **arch** dam survived intact.

Trouble ahead for the Three Gorges?

When it is completed in 2009, the enormous Three Gorges Dam on the Yangtze River in China will be the most powerful **hydro-electric** dam in the world. It will be 100 m high and 2 km long, and will create a reservoir 600 km long. It will make 10 per cent of China's electricity and also protect the lower Yangtze from the devastating floods that killed 300,000 people in the 20th century alone. But critics say that if the dam failed in an earthquake (earthquakes are common in the area), more than a million people would die. They believe that a series of small dams would be far safer.

Despite concerns, construction of the massive Three Gorges Dam in China continues.

Dam facts

The world's tallest dams

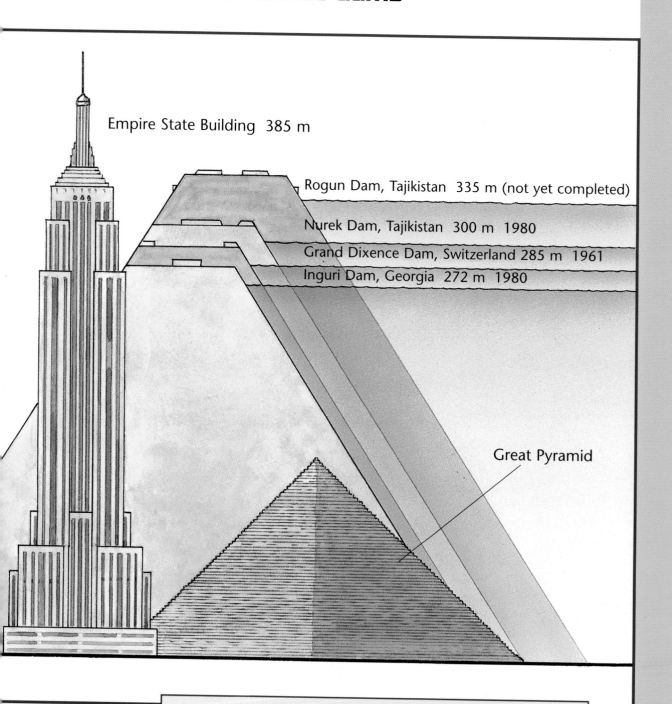

Empire State Building 385 m

Rogun Dam, Tajikistan 335 m (not yet completed)

Nurek Dam, Tajikistan 300 m 1980

Grand Dixence Dam, Switzerland 285 m 1961

Inguri Dam, Georgia 272 m 1980

Great Pyramid

The highest dams in the world would stand tall against other incredible structures.

FACTS ✚ The world's biggest dams

(The dams which have used most materials to build them)

Dam	Volume (cubic m)	Year completed
Syncrude **Tailings***, Canada	540,000,000	1992
Chapeton, Argentina	296,000,000	under construction
Pati, Argentina	230,000,000	under construction
New Cornelia Tailings, USA	209,500,000	1973
Tarbela, Pakistan	126,000,000	1977

*A tailings dam contains a **reservoir** of water and sludge pumped from mine workings. It is built from the waste material dug from the mine.

FACTS ✚ The world's most powerful hydro-electric dams

Power is measured in megawatts (MW). One MW lights about 20,000 light bulbs.

Dam	Power (MW)	Year completed
Itaipu, Brazil/Paraguay	12,600	1983
Grand Coulee, USA	10,800	1942
Guri, Venezuela	10,300	1986
Tucurui, Brazil	7690	1984
Savano-Shushenk, Russia	6400	1983

The Guri Dam in Venezuela is the world's third most powerful dam.

Glossary

arch type of structure that curves upwards (or backwards in the case of a dam) over an opening – it supports any weight above (or behind) the opening

Assyria ancient empire that flourished in the first millennium BC in the area known today as the Middle East

Babylonia ancient empire which flourished in the second millennium BC in the area known today as the Middle East

bedrock layers of hard, solid rock that are found in the Earth's surface and continue deep into the Earth's crust

borehole deep, narrow hole bored down into the ground to find out what earth and rocks lie below. Samples of earth and rocks are extracted from the hole.

buttress supporting wall. A buttress is built at an angle to the wall it supports, stopping the wall from falling over.

cement powdery substance that sets rock-hard after it is mixed with water. Cement is an ingredient in concrete.

climate the pattern of weather that a place has over a year

consulting engineer engineer who decides how a structure should be built

cut-off trench underneath a dam filled with waterproof material. A cut-off stops water seeping under the dam.

delta fan-shaped area of land formed where a river splits up and flows into the sea. The delta is built up by silt carried down the river.

downstream further down a river, in the direction the river is flowing

embankment bank with a flat top and sloping sides. It is built by piling up earth and rock.

engineer a person who designs or builds a structure

environmentalist person who is worried that human activities are damaging the natural environment

erode/erosion process by which water and wind are wearing away the rocks of the Earth's surface. Erosion can also wear away artificial structures such as dams.

estuary the area at the end of a river where it widens as it flows into the sea. Fresh water from the river mixes with sea water in an estuary.

fertilizer material which contains nutrients; it is added to soil to help plants to grow. Some fertilizers are natural and some are artificial.

formwork   metal or wooden moulds that concrete is poured into

geology   the study of rocks and how they are formed

generator   device similar to an electric motor – it creates electricity when its central core is spun round

geological survey   investigation to find out what layers of soil and rocks are under the ground

gravity   the force that tries to pull every object towards every other object. Gravity between you and the Earth pulls you down to the Earth's surface.

grout   a mixture of cement and water which is used to make earth or loose rock waterproof

hydro-electric power   power, normally in the form of electricity, made by letting water from a reservoir flow through a turbine. A generator attached to the turbine creates electricity.

Industrial Revolution   period in history (1750–1850) when industries such as iron-making began

irrigation   collecting water and making it flow to where it is needed to water growing crops

lock   step on a canal which allows ships to move uphill and downhill

Middle Ages   time in history between the 5th and 15th centuries AD

nutritious   describes substances, such as soil or food, which contain plenty of chemicals (called nutrients). These chemicals are needed for plant or animal growth.

ready-mixed concrete
concrete that is mixed at a concrete mixing plant and transported to a construction site in a truck

reinforced concrete   concrete that has steel reinforcing bars embedded in it

reservoir   artificial lake which forms behind a dam

seepage   water that trickles through the ground under or around a dam, or through an earth dam

seismic   to do with earthquakes

silt   made up of tiny particles of rock washed down a river; it is also known as sediment

spillway   chute that allows excess reservoir water to flow safely over or around a dam

tailings   dam containing a reservoir of water and sludge pumped from mine workings. It is built from the waste material dug from the mine.

turbine   wheel that is turned by flowing water. In a hydro-electric power station, water flowing down from the reservoir turns turbines which turn generators.

upstream   further up a river, in the opposite direction to the way a river is flowing

Index